Table of Contents

Climate Resistance Handbook

Or, I was part of a climate action. <u>Now what?</u>

⊲350

Published by Daniel Hunter. © 2019 Daniel Hunter. All images are used with permission, © 2019 350.org. Cover and back image by Daphne Philippoussis. Interior drawings are by J'ziah Cook (instagram @virgo_artistry) and Daphne Philippoussis (instagram @killed-mykactus)

ISBN #978-0-359-67267-7.

If you would like more printed copies of the *Climate Resistance Handbook,* please contact *Peace News* on 0207 278 3344 or promos@peacenews.info
Or order online: https://peacenews.info/webshop

350.org is an international movement of ordinary people working to end the age of fossil fuels and build a world of community-led renewable energy for all. Here's how we get there:

1. A Fast & Just Transition to 100% Renewable Energy for All. Accelerate the transition to a new, just, clean energy economy by supporting community-led energy solutions.

2. No New Fossil Fuel Projects Anywhere. Stop and ban all oil, coal and gas projects from being built through local resolutions and community resistance.

3. Not a Penny more for Dirty Energy. Cut off the social license and financing for fossil fuel companies — divest, desponsor and defund.

Join us at 350.org.

Foreword

(Greta has been striking from school every Friday, standing outside the Swedish parliament building and demanding better from her government. Her action struck a global nerve. Hundreds of thousands of students from over 100 countries have now joined the international school strike for climate.)

I don't want your hope. I don't want you to be hopeful. I want you to panic. I want you to feel the fear I feel every day. And then I want you to act.

Around the year 2030, we will be in a position where we set off an irreversible chain reaction beyond human control, that will most likely lead to the end of our civilisation as we know it. That is unless in that time, permanent and unprecedented changes in all aspects of society have taken place, including a reduction of CO_2 emissions by at least 50%.

And please note that these calculations are depending on inventions that have not yet been invented at scale, inventions that are supposed to clear the atmosphere of astronomical amounts of carbon dioxide.

Nor do these scientific calculations include already locked-in warming hidden by toxic air pollution. Nor the aspect of equity – or climate justice – clearly stated throughout the Paris agreement, which is absolutely necessary to make it work on a global scale.

We must also bear in mind that these are just calculations. Estimations. That means that these "points of no return" may occur a bit sooner or later than 2030. No one can know for sure. We can, however, be certain that they will occur approximately in these timeframes, because these calculations are not opinions or wild guesses.

People always tell me and the other millions of school strikers that we should be proud of ourselves for what we have accomplished. But the only thing that we need to look at is the emission curve. And I'm sorry, but it's still rising. That curve is the only thing we should look at.

Every time we make a decision we should ask ourselves; how will this decision affect that curve? We should no longer measure our wealth and success in the graph that shows economic growth, but in the curve that shows the emissions of greenhouse gases. We should no longer only ask: "Have we got enough money to go through with this?" but also: "Have we got enough of the carbon budget to spare to go through with this?" That should and must become the centre of our new currency.

The climate crisis is both the easiest and the hardest issue we have ever faced. The easiest because we know what we must do. We must stop the emissions of greenhouse gases. The hardest because our current economics are still totally dependent on burning fossil fuels, and thereby destroying ecosystems in order to create everlasting economic growth.

The basic problem is the same everywhere. And the basic problem is that basically nothing is being done to halt – or even slow – climate and ecological breakdown, despite all the beautiful words and promises.

I hope you will join me in acting. I hope this book helps give you a place to start and to keep going.

Because avoiding climate breakdown will require cathedral thinking. We must lay the foundation while we may not know exactly how to build the ceiling. We don't know exactly what we need to do.

But we have to take the next step. We have to act, to change the politics that allows this destruction to continue. We have to act urgently, because we simply have to find a way.

Introduction

I organised my first action in my quiet hometown. A group of us marched downtown. We sang songs. We chanted. We arrived at city hall. I hadn't thought through what it would look like to confront our mayor. So we showed up and gave impromptu messages. We triumphantly returned home, having delivered our message.

Since nobody does activism in my hometown, this was front-page news. I quivered with excitement as I read my quotes in the city newspaper.

The following days I had two strong — and different — feelings.

One feeling was proud excitement. I had a rush of adrenaline from the risks we had taken. I was proud of our song leaders. Our speakers. None of us had done anything like that before. I was proud of all of us who gave up time hanging with friends or catching up on schoolwork and, instead, participated in the action.

Over the next days, the glow of the action faded. I became aware of a second feeling. It was close to a stomach-clenching worry. I feared it wasn't enough or that the action hadn't worked as well as we had hoped. I saw that nothing immediately changed afterwards, even though we felt so powerful. I wondered if it was worth it. Doubt crept in.

I sat with two different feelings: the sense of success and the worry that we didn't really make a change. I could have given in to either of them. But instead, I began to wonder: *What's strategic here? How do my local actions add up to real changes? How do we move from one-time actions to a whole movement, where all kinds of people from all walks of life are joined together in common cause?*

This book is for those of you who, like me, have been part of an action and wanted to know: *What's next? How can I not only feel — but be — more powerful?*

The sense of urgency on climate has never been higher than now. We are in a serious crisis. If humans want to have a planet like the one we have lived on for millions of years, we have to adjust. We have to change. We have to do it quickly.

Thankfully, we have a wealth of elders to learn from. Regular people have changed the course of history. They have overthrown iron-fisted governments, fought for inclusion, for more democratic and fair systems. While those in power resisted, those with less power used social movements to force change.

We can learn from them that change does not happen just because an issue is important. People have to wage a struggle to fight for the Earth's climate. This is because the climate has an array of enemies: governments, corporations, media sources, and at times our own consumption and behavior.

So we need to bind together to create the strongest movement possible. Movements win because they channel the feelings of urgency, anger, fear — and our sense of this being wrong — into a force for change.

If you're with me, then this book is for you. Let's begin!

Chapter 1: Movements

HASHBAT HULAN WAS DISGUSTED WITH her government. The situation in the 1980s in Mongolia was harsh. Mongolians were ruled by a tough authoritarian government. The government crushed all dissent, leaving one political party — *their* party.

As a student, Hashbat decided to make a change. She met in secret with other young people. They discussed forcing a governmental change. Some said it couldn't be done. But Hashbat and others continued.

The young people were taking an enormous risk. They knew the government would use force to stop them. The government had nearly wiped out the whole Buddhist community. It had killed one out of five monks; most of the rest had fled. But Hashbat also knew people were tired of the current situation. Not just tired — angry and frustrated. That anger had no outlet until Hashbat and her friends came up with a public action.

On International Human Rights Day in 1989, the youth risked a protest. The government had carefully planned a series of speeches and military parades. It was in the great square, in the capital city of Ulaanbaatar.

The youth organised a group of about 200 people. The protestors stood with banners opposing the government's rule and chanted louder than the rock bands the government had paid for.

This got people's attention. The protestors were not the first to have this feeling. But they said it aloud. They gave voice to a feeling that had been kept silent by fear. At the time, most of the adults just whispered about the protests. Youth around the country copied them with marches of their own.

Hashbat then faced the question every movement faces over and over again: *What next?*

The youth took two paths quickly. The first was to create an organisational structure so they could make decisions and decide their goals. They also needed to choose tactics — the actions they thought would get them to their goal. They settled on a name — the Mongolian Democratic Union (MDU). They created a citizens' manifesto, with goals such as democratic elections in which any parties would be free to run.

They grew so large they needed a coordinating committee. They didn't want to operate like the government, with meetings in secret. So the MDU decided to hold open meetings — with over 1,000 members taking part.

The second decision was to switch tactics, and escalate. Doing the same tactics would become *routine*. They didn't want to be routine — they wanted to make possible what wasn't possible before. And they wanted tactics that would apply pressure on the government to give in to their demands.

It's like a game of tug of war. They had to keep applying more and more force in order to win.

The youth knew they were in a unique position. Most of the group's leaders were educated — some were even sons or daughters of government officials. Hashbat was the daughter of a government diplomat. That offered some level of protection. But they knew winning their demands would require sacrifice. Sacrifice meant they would have to take personal risks.

Their tactic: Go on a hunger strike until their demands were met.

Many of the youth activists had studied India, Russia, and China, where hunger strikes were sometimes successful, and sometimes not. It doesn't work if people don't know about it. So they held the hunger strikes in the public square — where everyone could witness them.

Hashbat and others started the hunger strike on March 7, 1990, at 2 pm, when the temperature in the square was -15 degrees Celsius. That really got people's attention.

They also knew they had to recruit allies. They reached out to a wide range of civil society groups. Five hundred workers at a nearby mine stopped work for one hour in solidarity. Monks joined and offered their support. Teachers went out on their own strikes.

Change was in the air. The pressure mounted on the government, which tried negotiations and offering weak compromises to stop the energy. But the youth — and now the other groups, too — refused to accept anything more than their core goals. This brought in more allies and opened up space for more tactics.

And they won. The government reluctantly announced democratic elections with all political parties able to participate. The struggle wasn't over, but the youth had won a huge victory.[1]

SOCIAL MOVEMENTS ARE LIKE A WAVE

There are lots of lessons on how social movements win in this story. *You win by using a range of tactics. You escalate so that you keep applying more force on your opposition. You win by ignoring the people who say you can't win. You organise allies, you sacrifice, and you keep active.*

One key lesson is they helped birth a *movement*.

Movements are forces of collective energy, carrying deep emotions like anger and love and moved by hopes and dreams for large-scale change. You know it's a movement because of the momentum and growing energy.

Movements are like a wave. They are a bundle of energy made up of many parts. The movement is not just one group or organisation. The MDU was joined by teachers, workers, and monks. Each group had its own part, its own methods, its own tactics. But the overall feeling was what made it a movement.

Movements are sometimes easier to see from afar (which is why, in this book, I tell stories both of climate justice movements and other social movements). When we're in the middle of a movement, it can look chaotic and disorderly. Movements are not clean. They are messy. And when inside them, we are painfully aware of their shortcomings.

Most people don't notice movements when they are small. Nobody in Mongolia knew how big that first protest was going to become. People only notice movements when the wave has gotten big enough.

This fact is important because it makes the humble work each of us does, however we are contributing, meaningful if we are in touch with the energy of the movement.

Understanding movements helps us understand how our actions are part of a bigger whole.

MYTHS OF SOCIAL MOVEMENTS

When we study movements, we have to face a problem: We have been lied to about how change happens.

Myth: Movements are lit like a match.
Movements don't appear from nowhere. The young people in Mongolia had met for months in secret. Before that, others had tried experiments but failed. The youth spent time learning from them (and others outside of Mongolia). Yet a history textbook might skip all of that and begin the story with thousands of people supporting the strikers. The myth that movements "suddenly appear" ignores the early stages. It ignores how we have to build up small networks. It makes *big* actions seem more important than the early, small ones. And it skips over skill-building and studying other movements.

Myth: Movements are built by heroic figurehead leaders.
When we think of famous movements, we may only think of Martin Luther King Jr., Mohandas Gandhi, or Nelson Mandela. But movements are more than heroic leaders. Some movements have them. Some don't. But all movements are built by many organisations, groups, and loose-knit networks that organise and act together for change. No organisation, action, or individual speaks for an entire movement.

Myth: Movements require complete internal unity.
People act as though past movements had a clear vision, a clear plan, and all agreed. But that was never the case. The young Mongolian activists argued and disagreed. They had internal splits about tactics and policies. Successful movements always have internal disagreements and division. Working for unity is great — and so is accepting the reality that we are not all going to see things the same way.

Myth: Petitions (or any single action) are a movement.
This myth goes like this: Want to stop the fossil fuel industry? Get a big petition! Or get everyone to do a social media share! Or a big march! But in reality, no single tactic is a movement. A movement

requires many different types of tactics. Some tactics, anyone can do. Others will require higher personal risk than most people are willing to take. Some tactics, maybe only some people can do, like a lawyer filing a lawsuit or the mine workers going out on strike. Movements require lots of different types of tactics — and relying on just one action will not result in change.

Myth: Movements succeed when they mobilise large, mass actions.
Countless times the refrain is heard: "We just need to have a giant march." However, movements don't win because of singular actions, however big. That can lead us to always try to organise big actions. Then we dismiss small actions, like those done in rural areas, communities who just joined us, or powerful but experimental tactics. And we can't just keep organising for the one big action. Movements need ongoing resistance — otherwise, the people in power can just wait until the event is over and continue ignoring movement requests. Movements require sustained pressure for change at many levels. It takes time to build, but without ongoing resistance, movements don't achieve their goals.

Myth: Movements only work in democratic countries, or where they don't have police repression.
Nonviolent social movements have overthrown powerful, oppressive regimes in the Philippines, Chile, Bolivia, Madagascar, Nepal, Czechoslovakia, Indonesia, Serbia, Mali and Ukraine, to name a few. Powerful social movements occur frequently in repressive countries. In democratic regimes, people may rely on traditional channels for advocating social change (courts, elections, etc). But in places with harsh rulers, they have saved a step: People already know those institutions won't save us. We have to organise ourselves. While organising looks very different from in democratic countries, groups have found ways to build movements even in the most repressive countries.

Myth: Movements need media attention to win.
This myth is common. And it's true that media can help influence public opinion. But it's not healthy for a movement to associate the health of the movement with how much media coverage it is getting . The Mongolian youth would have been very frustrated if they had to

rely on state-sponsored media to win. That's why they did their hunger strike in a public square. If we believe we are effective because the media are covering us, then what happens when the media get bored and decide to stop covering us? Movements are related to the people — and the media is just one avenue to speak to them.

Each of these myths makes us look outside of ourselves. We look for the heroic leader, the right circumstances, or what the newspapers say about us. That's not power. Movements are most effective when we look inward and find strength in ourselves and our relationships.

These myths help us see power in the wrong way. To see it the right way, we need to understand the *upside-down triangle*.

THE UPSIDE-DOWN TRIANGLE

The dominant view of power is that it flows from the top downward.

A student does what their teacher tells them to do. The teacher takes orders from the principal. The principal takes orders from their administrator. And so on, all the way up the pyramid to the head of state.

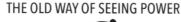

THE OLD WAY OF SEEING POWER

On climate change, we might see fossil fuel companies at the top. They buy our heads of state and leading politicians. Those politicians oversee government commissions that are supposed to regulate companies but instead violate land and workers' rights. Those commissions then approve the bosses' plans, who then order workers to clear land and dig oil out of the ground. And so on. In that view of society, everyone below follows orders from someone at the top.

But there's another way of helping groups view power: the upside-down triangle.[2]

THE UPSIDE-DOWN TRIANGLE

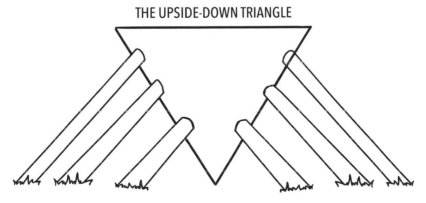

An upside-down triangle is always going to be unstable. An oppressive system that relies on destroying our planet is unstable. It's not natural to burn this much carbon dioxide (CO_2) and other greenhouse gases. The system needs to be held up by pillars of support.

The pillars make the structure seem legitimate and right. Pillars can be the laws, courts, media, and schools that train us to obey. Other pillars include people who may oppose the system but still help keep it running — including administrators, regulatory bodies, academics, and teachers — who refuse to speak out against what's wrong.

This view reveals how much *power* we actually have. The most repressive Mongolian government is forced to the negotiating table if its youngest citizens refuse to eat. If we don't comply, the system doesn't keep going.

Groups can use this tool to look at their work and develop a more complex and accurate understanding of power. Being able to see the *pillars of support* that keep bad policies in place can help expand our sense of how we can make change.

A group of young people in Serbia nonviolently fought their powerful, ruthless dictator in Serbia. They required every person who joined their movement to learn the upside-down triangle. They led trainings to explain the concept and their plan to remove the pillars they saw. They explained it this way:

By themselves, rulers cannot collect taxes, enforce repressive laws and regulations, keep trains running on time, prepare national budgets, direct traffic, manage ports, print money, repair roads, keep food supplied to the markets, make steel, build rockets, train the police and the army, issue postage stamps or even milk a cow. People provide these services to the ruler through a variety of organizations and institutions. If the people stop providing these skills, the ruler cannot rule.[3]

This approach was a key ingredient to their movement. And they were successful in overthrowing the brutal Serbian dictator.

This is one of the key insights from nonviolent direct action. Huge amounts of power live in us. We can make change by removing the pillars of support. When we remove our involvement, unjust systems become more unstable. And we can make them fall.

ANALYSING THE PILLARS OF SUPPORT

Let's look at the upside-down triangle of releasing carbon dioxide (CO_2) and other greenhouse gases. We can examine lots of pillars of support.

A few might include:

EXAMPLE PILLAR OF SUPPORT ON CO_2 AND OTHER GREENHOUSE GASES

The agricultural sector. Agriculture contributes to about 15% of global greenhouse gas emissions. The agribusiness industry is relentless in fighting for lower environmental and worker standards. Loss of forests is often caused by the pressure from agriculture and contributes a further 10% of greenhouse gas emissions.

Cars and the transportation sector. Transportation produces around 14% of all global greenhouse gases. This can also be a strategic issue. While people don't see CO_2 (or other greenhouse gases), they do see, smell, and taste pollution from cars and buses.

The fossil fuel industry. Burning fossil fuels is the single biggest cause of climate change: It causes the majority of all global emissions.

Governments that benefit from keeping it going. They reduce or scrap environmental laws or allow companies to break them. They have the power to make large systems change but keep giving up this power.

The list can get long quickly.

The number of opponents can make us feel overwhelmed, even hopeless. And there's a strategic insight here, too.

Rather than focusing on *all* the pillars of support at once, you can run a campaign — where you spend energy on moving *one* of them. Campaigns have the advantage of focus. In Serbia, the Otpor students ran campaigns moving key pillars of support they believed could move, including other youth, opposition politicians, and the police (!).

Focus is a gift of strategy. It helps us contribute our part, knowing others are doing other parts.

For example, 350.org has mainly focused on the pillar of the fossil fuel industry. We did so because the industry already owns over 2,795 gigatons of carbon dioxide in their reserves! That's five times more than the most conservative scientists believe we can put into the atmosphere (565 gigatons) and maintain *anything* like the climate we're used to.[4]

If they burn what they already have, we will blow past any hope of climate recovery. And their stock reports keep showing that's their plan. And even worse, they're spending billions in search of *more* oil and gas. In other words, they are a threat to all life.

So we targeted the fossil fuel industry. We did our own analysis of their pillars of support. What keeps that industry afloat?

We identified a few pillars we thought we could make an impact on: social licence, access, political permits, and finance. Our work became organised largely around *divestment* — a tactic of getting schools, houses of worship, and even big banks, cities, and countries to remove their investments from fossil fuels. Nobody should profit from their exploitation. So this is about finance.

But the divestment campaign is also about social licence — removing the public's acceptance by changing how the fossil fuel industry is viewed. Instead of seeing them as a needed profit-seeking company, the public is starting to see them as globally destructive monsters.

We also work to keep fossil fuels in the ground, allying with frontline communities globally who are protecting their lands. And then we keep hammering away at the social licence of the fossil fuel industry. They are not reasonable companies. They are entities willing to kill everything for profit. They should be thought of like slave traders and pirates — except neither of those ever threatened all life on the planet.

And what's good about picking a focus is that by winning one pillar, you can make others easier. The fossil fuel companies *buy off* governments — and so in many countries, we've campaigned to stop politicians from accepting any funds from them. When we weaken the fossil fuel industry, we weaken their ability to buy land and pollute water that's been care-taken by generations of indigenous peoples. Winning one pillar can help make other pillars easier.

Focusing on a pillar means you still get to talk about the whole system. But the focus means that instead of just asking "all the pillars to remove themselves" — you pick a pillar to really remove and crumble.

The Mongolian activists wouldn't have won if they had targeted everyone at once. Serbian activists didn't try to move *all* sectors of society at once — that would have spread them out too thin.

That's where it's great to be aware that movements are an ecosystem. *We* get to play our humble part in all of that.

A story from young people in Canada makes this even more clear.

POWER FLOWING FROM BELOW IN CANADA

A company called TransCanada was trying to build the Energy East pipeline. The proposal was to pump over 1.1 billion barrels *a day* from the tar sands, one of the dirtiest sources of oil. If built, it would be 4,000 kilometers long, across six provinces in Canada.

By 2014, the government was speeding up the approval process. The last big hurdle was the National Energy Board (NEB), a government body that was *supposed* to regulate pipelines. But mostly the NEB gives a green light to any bad project.

If people had accepted the power analysis of the NEB being the ones in power — then it was over.

But there was another way to think about the campaign: It's the people's decision, and we are the ones who decide if it goes ahead or not.

A group of young people strategised and launched a campaign called the *People's Intervention*.

The demand was simple: The NEB needs to consider the pipeline's *climate impacts*.

The strategy was easily understandable, too: *If* the National Energy Board wouldn't consider climate impacts, *they* (the people) would be forced to escalate with the People's Injunction and *prevent* the hearings from continuing.

The simple demand and understandable strategy made it easy for people to join. Soon, thousands of people were writing to the NEB asking for it consider climate impacts in its decision.

We call this an "if this, then that" strategy.

It's different from just asking someone else to do the right thing. And different from waiting around for them to do the wrong thing. It's taking the timeline into your hands — and explaining to everyone what the consequences will be if the bad policy happens.

It was also good organising, because people who were cynical about the government could sign the injunction. But people who trusted the government and believed it would do the right thing could join, too. And (this is important) they were signing up to do a riskier action *if* the NEB didn't do the right thing.

And that action had to be carried out — because the NEB did the wrong thing.

The NEB refused to accept people's input. It rejected over 2,000 comments from people talking about climate impacts.

A lot of new people were angry. Anger is good. And it needs a channel.

So at the next NEB hearing in Quebec, activists seized control of the meeting to plead for climate justice. Instead of letting the NEB tell people when they could speak, protestors stood up tall and shouted to make their voices heard. They were angry, and one person even threw themselves onto the table to halt the proceedings.

It was, after all, *their* government, and therefore *their* meeting.

The NEB freaked out. It shut the meeting down. It refused to hold more hearings.

This sparked even more outrage — and other pillars of support crumbled. Journalists turned up evidence of corruption. Indigenous leaders who were the first to oppose the pipeline organised a massive pan-continental treaty alliance against oil sands expansion on their traditional territory.

The pipeline's death was coming. Shortly after, the NEB collapsed under the pressure. It announced it would include climate impacts on the Energy East.

There was no way a huge pipeline could be called good for the climate. And TransCanada knew this. So three months later, Trans-Canada said it changed its mind due to "changed circumstances."

(No, they didn't admit they changed their mind due to protests. They rarely do.)

The campaigners won — by removing pillars of support and seeing how their actions could undo the power of the (apparently) most powerful forces in Canada.[5]

What they did, in essence, was run a campaign targeting a specific pillar of support (the NEB). And that helps us learn about the power of campaigns.

NEXT STEPS

Get handouts for teaching the Pillars of Support or Upside-Down Triangle at trainings.350.org.

Learn more about these concepts on the online skill-up course "How Movements Win" at trainings.350.org/online-skillups

Chapter 2: Campaigns

I WAS EIGHT WHEN I won my first *campaign* for the environment.

It was in the church where I grew up. After service, we had social time. People drank juice or coffee or tea and ate pastries. They drank from styrofoam cups. Then threw them away.

It was wasteful. For a few weeks, I brought my own reusable glass cup. I wanted to save the environment.

But that was a *personal* change. Each Sunday we threw away maybe a hundred styrofoam cups. I wanted to make a bigger change. A *structural* change.

So I got information. I found some allies in the church. An elder showed me that we already owned glass cups. Someone informed me that it was the leaders of the church (deacons) who were in charge of this kind of decision. These people convinced me to prepare a presentation and talk before the deacons. I researched how styrofoam takes centuries to decompose and statistics on how many are thrown away a year.

One afternoon I stood before the deacons. My knees shook. I trembled and dropped several of my notecards. I stuttered as I spoke.

I remember getting about halfway through when one of the deacons gestured for me to stop. I still remember my stomach clenching.

"You've convinced us," he said abruptly. He turned to the other deacons. "Can we just vote already?"

They voted yes to my proposal and moved to other agenda items.

At first, I was actually *disappointed*. I wanted to finish my presentation that I had worked so hard on. But that was just my fear talking. Once the shock was over, I realised: It was a victory! The church stopped using styrofoam cups and switched to glass!

What I had done was a basic campaign. The steps were all there:

RESEARCH • I learned about the issue and what changes needed to be made. It was important to get some facts behind me. But don't get bogged down trying to learn everything — be ready to act!

FIND OTHER PEOPLE • I couldn't have done it all alone. I simply didn't know enough. So I needed others who were sympathetic. Since it was a small campaign, it was a small group — only four people.

SET GOALS • If I had just said, "Save the planet," the deacons wouldn't have known what to do. The deacons needed me to show them what to do. They needed me to tell them exactly what change they should make. Goals are seriously important.

PRESSURE A BIGGER INSTITUTION • I was lucky that nobody came out against what I was saying. This campaign was unusually easy — partially because my goal was so small. But even still, making a structural impact is so much bigger than just a personal impact. That church still uses glass cups. That small act stopped over 150,000 styrofoam cups from being wasted. *Structural change* is almost always way more effective than *personal change* — like if I had simply gotten myself and a few friends to switch over!

IDENTIFY THE TARGET • I didn't just say "the church" should make a change. Our little crew found out who the deciders were — the deacons. Even as we told others about how important the campaign was, we knew it was the deacons who had to make the decision. In organising language, we call that a "target" — the person or people who can give you what you want. Knowing your target helps you design a campaign to persuade, pressure, or force them to do the right thing.

ACT! • I did something that scared me! That's pretty common in all campaigns, too. There is no social change without some risk.

CAMPAIGNS ARE EXPRESSIONS OF LOVE

A lot of people want to make change but don't know how. They therefore spend a lot of energy on a series of endless educational events or single actions that don't add up to anything.

    I could have done workshops about how we harm the environment. We could have watched movies every afternoon. Or maybe even done a vigil about "saving the environment." But those things don't, on their own, create change.

We need education. *But education without action is like planting a seed without watering it. We need to take action to make change.*

Campaigns use a lot of actions. They channel power by focusing on a concrete goal.

So campaigns start with a problem in society. But they don't end there. In campaigns, you identify a piece of what we want in the world and work toward achieving it. Having such a goal strengthens educational events, support services, and protests.

My campaign goal happened to be pretty small. And there are very big, so-called powerful organisations who believe in only campaigning on small goals. Sometimes they excuse themselves by saying they are being "realistic."

But accepting the current political reality of our times is a death sentence. Campaign goals do not have to be small, and they certainly do not have to be accepted as politically realistic.

This is another movement myth that has been taught. Campaigns are not based in "realism" but on the emotions of the people running them and their ability to connect with and convince others.

That was true for the Serbian activists. When they started, a lot of them were in high school. They were mocked by the press for claiming that they could overthrow Slobodan Milosevic, the country's leader.

It was true for black students in Soweto, South Africa in the 1970s. Leading government officials said that "Natives (blacks) must be taught from an early age that equality with Europeans (whites) is not for them."[6] That became policy under the Bantu Education Act. They faced brutal, cruel, and powerful white oppressors. And still they went out on strike. They took the first stabs at the pillars of support until, a few decades later, apartheid fell.

These dynamics are just as real today for the millions of global student strikers around the globe. Many are advocating for a Green New Deal or radical changes, while the political realists are certain it will not happen.

Campaigns change this dynamic in three ways. First, rather than broadly stating, "Radical changes are needed," campaigns set goals to lay out the steps to move forward. Society needs a blueprint, even if it may not implement it exactly as the activists say it should.

Second, campaigns use sustained actions to keep the pressure up. They move segments of society by using lots of different kinds of actions. No single action will convince people, so they try a variety of actions to move more people to their side.

Third, campaigns give people an outlet for their feelings. There is great anxiety across the world about climate change. Most people won't just go into the streets to express their feelings. Successful campaigns tap into those feelings. The goal gives people a sense that their actions will be meaningful.

That means we stay in touch with our most radical, heartfelt feelings. As one Otpor campaigner described, "We won because we love life more."

Campaigns, therefore, are more than just slogans or educational events. They use the power of a goal to pressure someone to make change.

REPLACE ENDLESS ACTIONS WITH GOALS

I was part of a group trying to stop the US war in Iraq. We were able to organise a march of 2,000 people in my city. That's a big turnout. And we got good press coverage.

So we did it again.

This time we got *10,000* people in the streets. I was one of the emcees for the rally and couldn't see to the end of the march. At that time, it was the largest march I had ever been part of organising. The feeling was amazing.

So what did we do next?

We didn't vary our tactics. We did it *again*. This time, we only got 1,500 people marching. And less press coverage.

Then how did we feel? Pretty bad.

And what did we do next?

Another march. Just a few hundred came this time — and virtually no press.

The problem was that we didn't really have a plan. We just had a *tactic*. So we kept using the tactic because that's what we knew.

We were doing *endless actions*.

ENDLESS ACTIONS

Imagine you're a politician, and you're the target of a campaign. People are outside your offices urging you to do something. You had to sneak in the back door so you wouldn't have to face them. You are feeling the pressure.

But will they be around the next day? Will they keep the pressure on?

If you can wait until the pressure is over, then you are unlikely to make the change.

Government officials (and most targets) regularly just wait until people do their big action. If the activists are lucky, the official gets some bad press for a few days. But the pressure does not stay. They wait until the heat blows over. Then they keep doing the bad thing.

VERSUS CAMPAIGNS

Campaigns vary up the actions. They recruit new people to support them. They sometimes use mass actions — where lots of people are involved. And other times, they pick very risky actions that only a smaller number of people will take part in. Each steps heads towards their target and winning their goal. They keep the pressure on.

Campaigns assess: Is our *capacity* growing? That doesn't just mean more people, but also stronger people — people with more skill, stronger relationships, more willingness to do riskier things — *and* more people.

With an issue like climate change — where to start? There are so many solutions needed — it's not just one. By forcing powerful players to do the right thing, we win over new allies and gain power for our movement for bigger and bigger wins. We have to build capacity to make change as quickly as we can.

Examples of other campaigns:

- New Zealand campaigners pressured their prime minister (the target) to stop all new off-shore oil drilling (the goal).
- 350 Georgia has run campaigns at the city level. Their first win came when the mayor of Kutaisi (the target) pledged to make their city 100% renewable by 2050 (the goal).
- In Kenya, a group of students found out about a 1,050 megawatt coal project on the coast and have organised to stop it (the goal) by pressuring the president, cabinet secretary and Ministry of Education (the targets).
- Mothers Out Front in the US wanted a "livable planet" for their kids but wondered how to turn this into a campaign. They decided on pressuring school districts (the target) to switch to electric school buses (the goal).

Campaigns make use of tactics. They may be a mix of small and big events, repeated or one-time actions. Unlike endless actions, campaigns have a goal and a target.

What's great about a campaign is that it can start small — but be part of a bigger thing. Mothers Out Front is a pretty small group. They got a few buses turned to electric. But the way they are campaigning is explicitly about climate change, about the ill effects of diesel fuel. And they advocate both *away* from diesel and *towards* renewable energy.

And small wins create momentum to keep people engaged, so you can move on to bigger wins.

In this sense, campaigns are more than the goal and target. *They are people's yearning for something better.*

People get used to oppression and low expectations. Campaigns shake us out of it. When people fight for something, they begin to believe they really deserve it.

When we campaign, we start to dream bigger. We begin to see that we can have agency in our world. We begin to expect better behavior from those around us.

Even when we lose a campaign, this energy lasts. That's part of why it's such a powerful way to structure our organising. It's easy to say, "Save the climate." It's harder to go to the Ministry of Education's office and say, "You have to stop the Lamu coal plant, because it will kill my children." The focus of campaigns is practice for us, our friends and our colleagues to get used to asking for more change, faster change — and to make it a regular practice.

Whereas endless actions could have us feel good, campaigns help us feel good *and* make a bigger impact.

HOW TO CREATE A CAMPAIGN

Some of us find campaigns because they are parts of a national movement. But when there's no national campaign to plug into, it's up to local groups to experiment and try stuff out. How to start?

Let's take a campaign from Jordan. It started with two young people: Omar and Hiba. While they had a few ideas, they weren't certain how two people could influence an issue as big as climate change.

They wanted to create a climate campaign that would feel relevant to other people. So they thought about what was important to people where they lived. They decided to target a sector of the economy that is one of the biggest causes of greenhouse gas emissions: transportation.

Jordan lacks a lot of public transportation infrastructure. That means many Jordanians purchase their own private cars. As a result, cities are congested and bursting at the seams. That wastes people's time, money and energy. And it causes massive environmental and health problems, with all the dirty air.

This is about climate change. But they could also get others involved because of the social, health, and economic dimensions. They picked a campaign with widely shared values to attract new people.

They had a sense of a campaign goal (better infrastructure for all of Jordan), but it wasn't detailed.

So they began researching. They read everything they could find about public transportation. And they began talking to friends and anyone they met about it. Slowly, they built a campaign group, *We Get Together: We are all entitled to public transport* (معاً معاً نصل – النقل العام حقنا جميعاً). They were no longer just one or two people. Their weekly meetings had about a dozen people meeting over tea and coffee.

They spent time outside bus stops and other public spaces listening to people's experiences. They recruited frustrated bus riders into the campaigning. And something they heard again and again was the need for a map to see how bus lines intersected and a schedule to have a realistic sense of when buses might arrive.

This helped them sharpen their goals. They decided to focus their campaign initially on Amman, the capital city. And among their goals was the creation of a map, app, and regular schedule for bus routes. In their case, they found out which were the government agencies that *should* have been creating these. Those were their targets.

It was not clear if they could win. But in every campaign, there comes a moment when you don't have all the information, but you take the risk and boldly tell people your plan, even when everything is not figured out.

Picking a campaign goal is also a tricky time. It can seem easier to "keep everyone in the group happy" by trying to work on everything and talk about everything. In my experience, groups that do this may hold people together for the short-term. But over time, people get frustrated that they don't see anything getting accomplished. They leave. And soon it becomes a tiny, irrelevant group.

They launched the campaign in a fun way. They held a public press conference, cleverly organized with people cycling towards the city's municipal building, symbolizing the goals.

It took many more tactics for them to get any wins (they held public events and outreach activities, co-launched a research institute, created their *own* maps…). But recently they won some victories: The city is adding money to public transportation, creating bus maps and apps to show bus routes, and improving coordination in public transportation. The group is still going, fighting for even more.

Their steps to build a campaign fit most I've been part of:
1. Gather a few people to meet
2. Decide on a problem you want to try to solve (and recruit more people)
3. Research the problem
4. Create a campaign goal, and figure out who is the target and how you want to move them (and recruit more people)
5. Launch the campaign (preferably in a fun way)

USE THE SPECTRUM OF ALLIES

None of us have figured out how to avoid and halt the devastating impacts of climate change. But we can learn from campaigns that have scored some key victories.

In Brazil, they were up against a corrupt government. The government was pushing hard to open the Amazon rainforest to oil drilling, using a technique called "fracking."

Let's just pause for a moment. The Amazon is our Earth's lungs. More than 20% of the globe's oxygen is produced in the Amazon rainforest. So fracking the Amazon is a very, *very* bad idea.

But it makes money for corporations. And it makes money for government officials in bed with them. And they can buy off lots of the public with that money, too.

So in 2015, the national government made plans to auction off rights to frack parts of the Amazon.

Activists resisting had only small groups of people ready to do something — mostly indigenous leaders. They needed a campaign strategy.

Organisers formed a coalition of parties, Não Fracking Brasil. They would organise across the country. They knew education was key. But education without action doesn't build a movement's power.

So along with every educational action was their campaign goal: getting local municipalities (cities, towns, states) to pass bans to stop fracking.

Their *target*: local city councils, which can pass the resolutions. The activists did not have enough power to win on the national level. But they could win on the local level. And they believed that people hearing about other people's wins creates momentum.

Their *goal*: to stop fracking by making it illegal, too expensive, and too unwelcome in Brazil. The bans were creative and legally enforceable. They made rules like, "No trucks carrying fracked oil, fracked water, fracked waste, or any fracking equipment can be on our city's roads." The bans increased the cost for fracking companies — and quickly.

This campaign approach increased capacity. It personalised the issue for people. It made local residents ask themselves, "Do you want fracking in your neighbourhood?" They accumulated dozens of local wins. After a city won, activists there would organise to move to the state level.

But some cities were very tough.

The city of Umuarama was one of those. Nearby cities had already passed the bans. But one local congressman was very pro-fracking. Two council members wrote a fracking ban. But the bill never moved forward.

Months went by, and they couldn't gain an inch. Then it got worse. One of the supportive council members was exposed as part of a (separate) corruption scandal.

Campaigners felt stuck. They kept meeting with the opposition council members. Nothing changed. And they kept rallying their base of supporters. Nothing changed.

In this local ban fight, how do we win?

They had a breakthrough. It's a lesson shown by the spectrum of allies.[7]

The spectrum of allies starts with a simple idea. There are people who are actively with you. They are your people (your base, your crew, your group, your active allies).

Then there are the people who are actively opposed to you. For Não Fracking Brasil, it was the most reluctant council members, fracking industry, and national government.

Campaigns make a mistake when they focus only on their active allies and active opposition.

Because *most* people aren't in either of those categories! The rest of the people might be broadly thought of as "the public." This tool is about breaking down the idea of "the public" and really seeing where our support lives.

SPECTRUM OF ALLIES

On the left side, we have our active allies. Active opponents are on the right.

In between might be *passive allies* or *passive opponents* — folks who might agree or disagree with you but aren't doing anything about it. Or they may be *neutrals* — truly undecided, completely uninformed, or truly apathetic.

The tool brings with it some good news. Campaigns don't succeed by getting everyone to agree with us!

Most successful campaigns never get their *active opposition* to change their minds. So let them go. Instead, support for their position is pulled away by shifting the *passives* and *neutrals* one step in our direction (for example, moving *neutrals* so that they become *passive allies*).

What a relief! We don't have to do it all.

The campaigners had to look outside of who was active on this issue. It became clear what needed to happen.

The campaigners saw that lots of religious leaders had been sitting on the sidelines. They hadn't done anything. So Não Fracking Brasil encouraged those neutrals by giving presentations and inviting them to public hearings. They also went to schools and community events.

The activists had some relationships with a few passive allies — some aldermen, archbishops, priests, the Rural Union president, and a well-respected Catholic bishop. They met with them one-on-one and said, "This is your time to get active!"

They moved people who had been neutrals and passive allies. Then they gave a public way for those people to show their support.

They organised a march from the Praça da Bíblia to City Hall. They timed it with the day the ban could be voted on. Thousands filled City Hall.

The numbers mattered. So did the optics of having a Catholic bishop lead the march. So did seeing members who had never shown up before.

The council was overwhelmed. Every council member voted for the ban — unanimously! Nobody wanted to be left out.

This campaign reaffirms the power of seeing the spectrum of allies.

Groups often waste a huge amount of time obsessing over the *active opposition*, even though they rarely move.

The spectrum of allies tool can be used in meetings to think about where people and groups stand on an issue. Healthy debates can emerge during this process, and it can expose our need for research. For example, *"Where does that union local stand on this issue?"* Debates may emerge about who to reach out to in order to help persuade other groups.

When using this tool, it's important to remind people to be specific. Instead of naming broad groups like "labor" or "children support groups," it's best to name specific groups or organisations. That's because the spectrum of allies is an *organising* tool — it's useful in figuring out who you are going to reach. That means the groups should be listed with names of people who can be contacted so you can reach out and engage with them.

The good news mentioned before is worth repeating. We don't need to convince everyone to become active allies to achieve our goals. Take the abolitionist movement against slavery in the United States, as an example. If you add up every petition signed, every meeting, every public action — not even 1% of the population were *active allies*. Yet the movement was successful.

We therefore don't have to become hyper-focused on moving our *active opponents*. Our work is to steadily move *passive allies, neutrals,* and *passive opponents* in our direction. We keep our *active allies* engaged.

As of this writing, the Brazilian coalition has managed to get 400 municipalities to enact some ban to halt fracking.[8] States are now passing bans. And support for fracking at the national level is cracking.

MOVE THE ROCK

Sometimes when groups decide to pick governments as their target, they fall into the trap of thinking like lobbyists. *Lobbyists* don't focus on what the public wants. They have private meetings, expensive dinners, and fancy events to persuade government officials. If that fails, they'll just line officials' pockets.

Fossil fuel companies have spent millions on lobbying. They're *very* experienced at that. That is *their* domain.

So what's the movement's way of changing governments' minds?

It's by seeing politicians as a balloon.

A balloon floats in the wind. If you blow on it, it can be pushed one way or the other. It *follows* the wind, like politicians who can change their opinions and stances easily.

But politicians are tied to a rock. If we swat at them, they may sway to the left or the right. But, tied down, they can only go so far. Instead of batting at them, we should move the rock: people's activated social values.

Depending on our government, the string might be longer or shorter. But politicians know they can only be pushed so far one way or the other. If they absolutely violate social norms, they are in trouble.

This is critical.

For example, I didn't think very much about climate change a number of years ago. I *cared* about the environment. And if you asked me, I'd tell you I *cared* about climate change. So I had the value — *but it wasn't activated.*

I didn't really need someone to teach me about the issue. I needed someone to get me *active,* so that I was engaging politicians, my neighbors, colleagues, friends. When a friend asked me if I wanted to help them join a campaign on climate change — I said yes. I became activated. Our goal in moving the rock is to build campaigns that encourage people to *act* on their values.

When we move the rock, it pulls all the politicians towards us — without having to pressure each one separately.

POLITICIANS ARE LIKE A BALLOON

If you think about politicians this way, two things change.

The first is that you realise they are not, under even the most autocratic system, all-powerful. They have a constituency they have to keep in place — people whose support they need. (That's a reminder about the pillars of support.)

The second is that we could spend all our energy swatting at the politicians. *But* the lesson from Umuarama is this: The activists stopped trying to just swat the politicians, the balloon. They needed to move the rock — and that means *activating* the values that people have.

People can believe something. But if they don't act on it, politicians won't care.

The point is this: If your target is a politician, don't spend all your time just trying to *convince* them to change their minds. Feel free to try for a short while. But if you're still stuck, then recall that the more *efficient* way to move them — and other politicians, too — is to use the campaign to change what politicians think the political risks and possibilities are for them. You do that by moving the rock.

This is how movements win. We move more and more people onto our side. As we run successful campaigns, we grow the energy of the whole movement — getting more interest, more excitement. And then we have to deal with a different problem for the next chapter: growth.

NEXT STEPS

Get handouts for the Spectrum of Allies and How to Build a Campaign at trainings.350.org.

Learn more about these concepts on the online skill-up course "Intro to Campaigning 101" at trainings.350.org/online-skillups

Chapter 3: Growth

ORGANISERS ALMOST ALWAYS HAVE AN endless list of to-do's. We have so many things to track. *Who to call next. When to announce the next campaign. The website needs fixing. There's a conflict in the group that needs addressing.*

And few things make that list longer than a successful action! After the action is over, there's a ton more things to plan. *More* people want to help out. *More* demands are placed on the organiser.

What makes a good organiser *isn't* someone who has completed their to-do list. It's someone who can manage that list with grace. It's someone who makes good choices about which things they do next.

And being a good organiser means finding new people to help out with that list.

That means we have to develop a structure to *grow*. We need a way to absorb that energy and turn it into more capacity.

Your group might be a formal organisation with a structure, board and funders (like the Brazil campaign). Or it might be a a loose network (like the Mongolian youth organisation). Or it might be a few friends (like my anti-styrofoam campaign).

But it needs a way to handle that growth.

Take the US Civil Rights movement, right after the launch of the sit-in movement in February 1960. The campaign kicked off with four black men sitting at a segregated lunch counter. They were violently refused service.

Within weeks, the student sit-in movement had grown across the country. Some groups had successes. Some groups faced failure at the hand of brutal mobs. But hundreds of young people, black and white, were joining the sit-ins and experimenting with that campaign model.

This caught the attention of national Civil Rights movement

leaders, like Ella Baker. Ella Baker was a long-time organiser who listened to what was happening at the grassroots. She had made her own name for herself, organising campaigns for school reform and civil and women's rights across the US. She was an organiser in the best sense: following the energy of the people, building up leaders, and always with an attitude of, "If we build strong leaders, we don't need strong organisations."

She was then working at Dr. Martin Luther King Jr.'s organisation, the Southern Christian Leadership Conference (SCLC). She alerted Dr. King about the sit-in movement.

The young people represented a new energy. They were disciplined and nonviolent, with escalated tactics. They didn't believe in a single leader, and so they rotated who facilitated meetings. They were bold. They were inspiring and made waves. They injected new energy and urgency into the movement.

They were also chaotic and unorganized. They were unclear on direction and with little relationship to each other.

So when Ella Baker convinced Dr. King to pull together a national gathering of the sit-in leaders, some were nervous. They worried they would be taken over by the older and more cautious groups. They knew the mainstream groups expected to be respected.

Dr. King also had to be convinced, because he had his own concerns. The young sit-in leaders benefited enormously from the work he and others had been doing. Those leaders and Civil Rights movement activists had tilled ground for the seeds the sit-in organisers were planting. Dr. King had made enormous personal sacrifices and made in-roads into previously hostile territory. He knew the sit-in movement couldn't have taken hold without the media attention and allies that his earlier campaigns helped generate. (In fact, sit-ins that had happened years earlier never caught fire.)

Many of the sit-in leaders idolised Dr. King. But others mocked him. They called him "Da Lawd," and some joked about his careful approach. Dr. King worried that their sense that they had all the answers meant they would not work well with others.

These generational tensions are common dynamics in movements. We can relax when we see it. It happens. When it doesn't become overly personal and mean, it can inspire growth.

The meeting went ahead. Dr. King spoke. Other elders of the movement spoke. The unspoken goal was to organise the young people *into* Dr. King's organisation, the SCLC.

Ella Baker moved beyond just her organisational role. She privately urged the students to develop their own organisation. She sensed their energy would be drained if they followed into the more stodgy SCLC.

She organised leaders in local SCLC chapters to send money and give official (and often unofficial) support to the sit-in organisers. And she spent hours over the nights talking with the sit-in leaders about what kind of movement structure they wanted to build.

The sit-in organisers decided on a structure and a name. They decided not to use the top-down structure of SCLC with its iconic Dr. King. Instead, they would rotate leaders and have everyone present at group meetings (which often meant their meetings ended late into the next morning!). They decided to be the Student Nonviolent Coordinating Committee — a name now known for winning key legislation to make sure blacks would be allowed to vote and stop vote suppression tactics.[9]

MOVEMENTS NEED A STRUCTURE

Ella Baker showed some key lessons on being an ally to the movement. She didn't direct, but she didn't *only* follow. She didn't move based on *her* organisational role, but she listened for what *this* group of young people wanted to do. She *did* look ahead and see what they would need before they knew. She organised a chance to get together, protection from being overtaken, resources, and coaching on some of the details. (In her case, she soon quit SCLC and joined up with SNCC.)

But that need to create a *structure* is important for all movement groups.

The Fossil Fuel Divestment Student Network, in the US, was facing the challenge that the sit-in movement faced. They needed a structure to move forward.

Local campaigns to get campuses to divest from fossil fuels were running, doing their thing. Some were great. Some were amazing. Some were so-so. Some struggled.

But there was no way for the movement, as a whole, to learn from each other. No way to develop their own learning curves and make changes to their overall strategy.

Becca Rast, one of the youth organisers, explains: "We needed to create an organisation for *students* to learn, grow, and train." To ensure this, they created a *National Coordinating Body* for the Divestment Student Network made up of active students. The coordinating body helped the youth-led movement stay youth-led.

The roles were clarified to minimise confusion (though there's always some confusion). The national body would not determine local strategy or structure. It would decide national actions. It would select national spokespeople. It would organise national gatherings and set up trainings, which locals could choose to attend or not.

This fit with their culture. The US student divestment culture wouldn't have gone with a very top-down structure. But it needed to be clear enough that it could move their work forward.

And the structure paid off.

Within their first year, the students were part of a national march. The march was part of a broader coalition. But the youth turnout was huge: 50,000 people. The local bodies had their heads in their local campaigns. But the national coordinating body had been preparing for that moment.

The day before the march, they organised divestment workshops as part of a youth gathering. They signed up as many of the youth as they could reach to join the national movement (and join local campaigns, too). The followed it up immediately with eight trainings held around the country on topics like the upside-down triangle, how to organise, the just transition framework, and anti-racism workshops.

The energy of their national gatherings flowed back into the locals. Eventually, the number of locals grew. They had to add another layer — regional — between the national and the local. Some people call this structure the *snowflake* model, because of how it looks.

No matter what structure you use, there are some lessons in this story to help any group get better at absorbing new people.

ACT-RECRUIT-TRAIN

One of the models the Divestment Student Network taught is the "Act-Recruit-Train" model.[10]

We do an action (and we'll talk more about those in the next chapter). Then what? We have a lot of people who want to get more involved!

So right after (and during!) a big action, we recruit them. Recruitment is something you do, not something that you get people to do. So don't tell people to sign up — whip out a phone and have them join. Pass out sign-up sheets at every action, and get someone to type them into your contact lists. Have a bunch of computers set up where people can volunteer for specific tasks.

Right after the large People's Climate March, the students had a plan for organising the thousands who arrived. One of the lead local Swarthmore College chapters, for example, organised about 200 people to go to the march. On the return trip buses, the organisers handed out flyers to people to join their training just *four* days after the major march.

Why this model?

There's a phrase, "Strike while the iron is hot." That's some of the best organising advice you'll get.

People join something when they're energetic about it. If you wait two weeks, they'll have other things on their mind. You want to capture their energy and give them an outlet for it right away. You do this knowing some people will not follow through. But you're going to try to keep as many people as possible from the action involved — otherwise they will fall back into their regular life and not into the campaign.

Out of the 200 who went to New York City with the Swarthmore students, 50 people came to the training. And then three of them went on to join the core of the local group.

One reason training is so important: Training is teaching and learning. It's a way to pass along skills and political frameworks, develop leaders, and share the work more equitably. Without training, our movement has a low learning curve. And then our movement can't adjust to the changes in politics and our opponents' tactics.

Wherever you plan an action (or a training, or a recruitment strategy), it's helpful to look ahead and make sure you have planned the Act-Recruit-Train cycle. With it, you can rapidly bring in new people.

WINDOW SHADE THEORY OF LEADERSHIP

Clarity about roles and who makes which decisions is very helpful. In the Divestment Student Network, they created a national body that had clear boundaries. *It dealt with national issues. It didn't determine local strategy. And so on.*

One way to view these boundaries is with the window shade theory.

Let's say you're a volunteer in a local group. The part of the window covered by the window shade is the part that you cannot do without permission. Maybe you can't send out fundraising letters without checking in with the leader. The rest of the window, the part not covered by the window shade, is what you can do without permission. Maybe you can collect petition signatures and write Facebook posts.

WINDOW SHADE THEORY OF LEADERSHIP

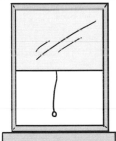

In the vast majority of groups, this window shade is never defined. In that case, the window shade goes up and down depending on the leader. Maybe the leader is feeling relaxed and open, and the window shade comes up. So the volunteers can do a lot on their own.

Or maybe an action went poorly, and now the leader is feeling more controlling. They take the window shade down.

One of the quickest ways to burn out volunteers (and each other) is to keep moving the window shade up and down on each other.

Whether you're a national body or a local leader, it's helpful to list out what actions people can take on their own. Then proceed to let them go to it!

IDENTIFY THE CORE VALUES OF "US"

There's often a lack of clarity about movement structures. That's because we're based on values — not paid membership, or job title, or a formal structure.

Who gets to say they are part of your group? Who can represent the group to the media? To politicians? To funders?

At its heart: "Who are we?"

I remember a meeting of a local group where I live called Earth Quaker Action Team. At that meeting one member threw up her hands: "Am I part of Earth Quaker Action Team or not?" It's a common scene replayed in many movements.

Who are *we*.

At the time, I replied simply, saying, "Yes, if you stand for our campaign goal and will work with us to make it happen, then you're part of the *us*." That wasn't a full answer. I should have taken more time with her and explained our values. We believed in nonviolent direct action (and that meant we didn't do traditional electoral work). We were not all Quakers, but we leaned on that faith tradition. And so on…

In other words, I should take the time to help answer the questions of who we are and the values we stand for. How do we relate to frontline communities? How do we talk about justice and equality?

I've seen lots of processes to try to work these questions out. And the thing that seems to work the best is lots of face-to-face conversations to talk them through.

Some people create a mission statement to introduce these concepts to people. Others rely solely on informal and oral channels. But you need to help people understand what it takes to be inside the movement — so they can be proudly part of you.

THE LADDER OF ENGAGEMENT

Growing groups face a challenge. *Organisers are often the ones doing much of the work of the group — and they get tired of doing everything.*

They set up the Act-Recruit-Train model. They think about the
window shade for new recruits. And they share their core values with
new people.

One option for the organisers getting tired is they keep sacrificing
more and more. They give up sleep. They sacrifice school and work.
They stop social activities — it always becomes about the activism.

For most people, that's just not sustainable.

So what's the alternative?

Getting new people to step into leadership.

A story from Ferrial Adam in South Africa provides us an example.[11] She was part of an environmental justice organisation working
with folks at the grassroots. Led largely by women, they were chal-
lenging a government policy called "Free Basic Electricity." That
policy guarantees the government will pay for a certain amount of
electricity to poorer households (currently 50 kWh, about 5% of what
the average US home uses).

This is a major issue, as the lack of access to energy often dooms
whole districts to poverty. For example, those lacking electricity often
rely on carbon-intensive paraffin, candles, or cutting down trees. This
leads to a host of negative environmental and health effects.

This policy was widely credited as a successful social justice
policy. But those who were most impacted by this policy weren't part
of the debate. So Ferrial began a research study to learn more about
the actual impacts this had for households, which meant going to the
poor districts in the city of Johannesburg.

She started where the people were. Her first step was finding a
group of women who were keen and already working on energy
struggles. It was important to start by explaining the intention and
need for the work. She started by getting people to monitor their use
of electricity. She spent time building relationships with mostly
women, who ran the households. It took many months of weekly
workshops to teach people to calculate the energy consumption of
different household items.

Her report was done. And she could have been the person pre-
senting the report in front of national bodies. But when public
hearings were planned to increase costs, the people Ferrial had been
working with wanted more. She asked the women if they would

testify on their own behalf. They jumped at the chance. Ferrial says, "It was so amazing and powerful watching people go to a hearing and speak as a collective on why the government should not raise the price of electricity."

They became part of the organisation and took their own leadership. Ferrial wasn't calculating people's consumption for them *and* writing the report *and* talking before the national bodies. She was organising. She wasn't doing things that people could do for themselves.

The women were supported through steps of engagement over the months. This way, they gained expertise about their own electricity usage and education on national policy and the impacts of climate change. Each step gave them increased confidence to not only testify but be strong community activists.

LADDER OF ENGAGEMENT

This concept is called the "ladder of engagement."

The women wouldn't have been ready to testify *as their first step*. Instead, they needed to learn more about their own situation. Then they needed to connect to others' stories and see they weren't alone.

The ladder helps us think about what to do when people say, *"What you're doing is great, how can I help?"*

In our minds, we have our to-do list and things we need done. But that's not where to start. We have to think from the perspective of that person. That probably means our first response is, "Let's talk about what you're up for doing." And we find out what kinds of tasks they might be willing to help us with — ones that match *their* interest and involvement (not our long to-do list).

This isn't a science, and each person is different. Some people have absolute terror making phone calls but would happily risk civil disobedience. So chatting with people about their interests is important.

Thinking about newer activists in our group with the ladder of engagement in mind helps us think about the next step for them. And as Ferrial did, we can offer steps to keep increasing their level of commitment and involvement. This cultivates relationships and helps people move up the ladder of engagement, which is how you, too, will increase your group's involvement.[12]

RECRUIT PEOPLE OUTSIDE YOUR CIRCLE

Of course, to get more people into leadership, you have to have lots of conversations with them — about the goals of the campaign and the work you're doing. You have to build trust.

And you have to find them!

Sometimes it's hard to recruit new people, because we get used to talking the same way about an issue. You may have some ways you talk about climate change that you're used to.

But someone you want to recruit may not talk about it that way.

They may not care about climate change, but they may care about cats. You can tell them that climate change is increasing the habitat for fleas, ticks and mosquitoes. That's bad news for pets. It exposes them to new diseases, like West Nile, Lyme disease and heartworm.

Or maybe they care about football. Climate change isn't going to end football soon, but it will change the game. With more erratic climactic events, you will see more games like the snowy 2013 World Cup qualifying match between USA and Costa Rica. It was a disaster. Or, since the spread of Zika (and other diseases) increase with the rise of temperatures, Brazil's warmer temperatures threatened to derail the Rio 2016 Olympics.

Or maybe they just don't like being angry! A study on climate and conflict showed that warmer temperatures increase people's personal conflicts (by 2% amongst friends, and by 11% outside their social circle). So hot temperatures can cause more anger.

But even when we get more flexible in talking about climate change, many groups often mistakenly believe they've tapped all the people who are passionate about their issue. *"Nobody in my school cares about climate change."* The problem is often not that we have exhausted the possibilities in our city or small town — it's how we are organising.

When it comes to recruitment, many of us think of people just as individuals. We imagine there is a scattering of people out there from whom to recruit (left side of image).

SEEING SOCIETY AS INDIVIDUALS OR SOCIAL CIRCLES

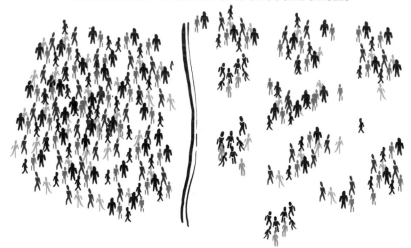

The reality is different. Most people are not attracted to groups simply as individuals. Ask around, and you'll find that very few people get involved in a cause because they receive a flyer, get sent an e-mail, see a poster, or see a Facebook post. Most people join a group or get involved because someone they know personally invited them. That's because society is better understood as clusters of "social circles" (right side of image).

Social circles may be organised as formal or informal groups —

religious communities, gangs, tight-knit neighbourhoods, etc. Social media can show you the number of people who are friends of friends many times over.

The quickest way to build a group is to ask people in your networks of friends or family. Those people are the most likely to say yes to you. But a group stops growing when it reaches its maximum potential of people from its members' initial social circle. Continuing to reach out within that circle may not bring in many more people. The trick is to jump out of your social circle and find people connected with other social circles.

Some ways to do this:

- *Show up at the events and meetings of people outside your circle.* This is a great chance to meet others, see how they work, and find out where their values overlap with your campaign.
- *Stop doing the tactics you've always been doing, and try new ones that might appeal to different audiences.* If your tactics are marches, strikes, and massive, disruptive direct actions, and it's not working, then it's time to adapt. Ritualising our actions makes us predictable and boring. People want to join fresh and interesting groups.
- *Notice when other groups make overtures toward your movement, and follow up with them.* For example, if we are seeing reluctant corporate and government allies taking steps towards us, maybe with some of them there are relationships we can build to keep them moving faster.
- *Do lots of one-on-one meet-ups with leaders from other movements and groups.* Meet with different people — not to recruit them, but to learn from them. *What are their values? What interests them? What strategies recruit people like them?*
- *Do direct service.* Gandhi was a big fan of what he called the "constructive program," which means not only campaigning against what we don't want, but also building the alternative that we do want. Climate disasters provide large-scale and small-scale chances for us to be part of that. Direct service to disaster survivors and other community-based projects put us

shoulder to shoulder with others who want to make things better. Who better to hear a pitch about joining your campaign?

Growing outside of your social circle takes time, but when it comes to building successful groups, it's worth the effort.

NEXT STEPS

Get handouts for the ladder of engagement, recruiting outside your circle, and how to build a base: using one-on-ones at trainings.350.org.

Learn more about these concepts on the online skill-up courses "Having Climate Change Conversations" and "Intro to Campaigning 101" at trainings.350.org/online-skillups

Chapter 4: Tactics

I LOVE THINKING ABOUT TACTICS. Tactics are actions or events we organise, like marches or strikes or sit-ins. Here, I'll use the words *actions* or *tactics* to mean the same thing.

Some people think that tactics are the building blocks of campaigns. But I don't believe that's true. I believe *relationships* are the building blocks of campaigns.

What tactics do is give an expression to the feelings we carry in those relationships. Tactics carry with them a tone. *Are we angry? Are we feeling light-hearted? Are we feeling urgent and serious?*

Tactics are really like a kind of broad communication. They communicate with the broader audience — those people on different parts of the spectrum of allies. They are how we move from just *thinking* or *believing* something to carrying it out.

They are, therefore, also about power. Tactics are where we show our power and, in that way, try to pressure our opponents into doing the right thing.

Yotam Marom is an experienced organiser and was a leader in the Occupy movement, which began with an occupation in New York City's Wall Street financial district. The Occupy movement exposed the dissatisfaction with the current economic system and laid blame squarely on the 1% who own and control the levers of politics and economic systems.

He's written about some of the shortcomings of that movement, including some important reflections on tactics:

> A big part of what made Occupy Wall Street work was the occupation. It created a way to capture our anger and vision, brought people together, and gave people a reason to learn about organizing. It pointed a finger at our opponent, and broke the rules of business as usual. And it was spreadable -- so anyone could become part of the movement, at least in theory.

But it was part of our undoing as well. We were wed to a single tactic, and that made us less flexible. The tactic was hard to maintain, it took enormous energy, and it didn't always match local contexts. Our occupation a few blocks away from the bull on Wall street tells a particular story, but what does an occupation of a parking lot outside a grocery store in Indiana tell?

Because we had relied on it too strongly, we hadn't developed any other effective ways to recruit and organize people. In other words, the tactic became the movement. It lost its meaning to the public, and it also gave our enemy a clear way to take us apart. If the tactic becomes the movement, all you have to do is kill the tactic and the movement goes with it.

Movements that get too associated with a single tactic lose the ability to improvise. Anyone can get too used to whatever we know. And doing something new is risky. If we do something different, we may not be seen in a positive light, or we may lose some people who liked the old thing we were doing.

But using the same tactics over and over again usually gives us similar (or smaller) results. And change requires shaking things up.

In one group I worked with, we made a vow to never do a march or rally. Why? Because we wanted to stay fresh. We wanted to make sure that our *opponents* had never seen anything like us before. We wanted to keep them off-balance and never knowing what to expect from us. So we created dozens of new actions (and, in truth, we did a few marches and rallies).

So here are just a few examples of tactics you may not have heard of:

THE HONK-IN • In Lebanon, citizens honked their horns at members of parliament to tell them, "Your time is over." The tactic grew until wherever the MPs went they were honked at. Some changed license plates to try to avoid being honked at everywhere.

STRIPPING NAKED • In northern Uganda, there have been ongoing land disputes since the days of colonialism. A rich businessman illegally claimed ownership of land. Protests erupted. Police were called and sided with the businessman. The local community made a roadblock. The police and military soldiers tried to push through.

That's when several elder women stripped naked. This is a powerful cultural curse, a thing of shame to see. On sight, the minister involved in the deal broke into tears and pleaded. Soon after, the community regained title of their land (and some of the soldiers apologised).[13]

PICKETING POLICE HOUSES • Members of the movement organisation Otpor, in Serbia, were regularly beaten up by police in their quest to kick out the dictator Milosevic. As a tactic to try to move the police to their side, they enlarged photos of injuries made by police. They carried these photos outside the homes of the offending police officers, so their neighbours could see what they were up to.

And Otpor even escalated that tactic. They would found the school that the most brutal police officers' children attended. They go there with signs and ask the schoolchildren, "They're beating up young people like us, is that okay?"

This applied social pressure and resulted in police eventually disobeying orders and hastening the overthrow of dictator Milosevic.[14]

TWITTER DEBATE • In Kenya, a group fighting the Lamu coal plant hosted a "twitter debate." At an appointed hour, organisers would propose a topic. Then their members would debate the issue over twitter. This allowed people from different universities to participate at the same time. It was a chance to see people's arguments. And it increased members' knowledge and prepared them to bring new people into the movement.[15]

FRACKING MAGIC • The campaign against fracking in Brazil escalated. When the government tried to auction some of the land for fracking, the organisers came up with a wild idea. Magicians make impossible things happen. They figured the government officials were pretending to be magicians by saying that you could frack the Amazon rainforest and not destroy the environment. So they decided they would interrupt the auction and do magic tricks and throw magical glitter over the proceedings. (They almost did it — when the government got word of the action and negotiated a settlement. The organisers deemed the agreement a big success.)[16]

ACTIONS HAVE A TONE

All of these actions have a tone.

While the Brazilian anti-fracking activists were being sarcastic and funny, the Ugandan land activists were being very serious. Can you imagine being the Otpor activists staged outside of the houses of police who had beaten you up? This required them to be very brave — and they did it in a very serious, even defiant and angry way.

As you're developing a tactic, you can pick your tone. This is a way that movements express the feelings of the people.

Take a simple march. It's a tactic where people go from one place to another place.

But the tone can be very different:

WATER IS LIFE • Canadian protestors decided to pressure their newly elected Prime Minister Justin Trudeau. It was just a few days after he was elected. But they didn't want to wait around. They wanted to pressure him right away. So over several days, they stood outside his residence, asking him to become a climate champion.

On each day, the protests were led by prayers from indigenous leaders. On the third day, the protestors carried water with them. The water came from vulnerable areas where fossil fuel companies wanted to exploit the land. Tearful prayers and heart-filled stories of the water echoed as people marched to Trudeau's residence.

The tone was somber.[17]

RAISE THE HEAT • In Australia, there was a major fight to stop nine new coal plants in the Galilee Basin. With a hostile government and well-connected coal companies, it would be hard to stop. Protestors decided that in order to stop the plants, they would target the banks funding the projects.

One of the biggest was CommBank. And during a week of "Raise the Heat" actions, protestors in the city of Canberra donned black formal clothing and yellow scarves or hats. They brought along percussion instruments for a lively march to the CommBank offices. And they brought a coffin full of fake coal — to symbolise this dead investment.

The action had music and was a mix of serious but also hopeful. The tone was future-oriented and stating the positive vision of a world without coal.[18]

DRACULA STRATEGY • In France, pressure was mounting to scrap any new fossil fuel projects. Protestors had just waged a multi-year campaign to halt fracking and were ready for more. So activists saw a chance when the fossil fuel companies hosted a major summit on off-shore drilling. All the big fossil fuel companies would be there, like Total, Shell, BP, and Exxon Mobil.

350 organiser Nicolas Haeringer describes their strategy as "Les vampires sont tués par lumière," which means "Vampires are killed by light." They decided to be highly confrontational to raise the profile of all these vile companies meeting. Activists planned sit-ins and major blockades. They added marches to the mix, some building up to attempts to get past police barriers and get into the meetings.

In this context, marches were confrontational, even angry. The tone was defiance and anger.[19]

THE THREATENING THANK YOU • I was part of a campaign where our reluctant City Council had done (nearly) everything we asked of them. It was strange, because they were definitely not allies. But they felt our pressure and so gave in to our demands.

At the end of the year, we wanted an action to let them know the pressure was still on them. But it wasn't like they were a hostile target. So what did we do?

We created cardboard "Standing with the People" awards. We made one for each City Council member. We marched outside City Hall — then entered City Council during their regular proceedings. We interrupted the meeting by shouting down the head of council. We announced we were giving them awards! We quickly gave each councilmember their own award, before the police escorted us all out.

It was a message of encouragement and a threat. The tone was kind, laced with warning.

As you can see, the same tactic can easily have a wide range of tones.

You can pick the tone through the symbols, actions, speakers, and framing of the action. In this way, you can connect to the feeling of the people you are organising — because actions are about expression of what is inside of people.

This is important, because the issue of climate disaster always has feelings of despair somewhere in the mix. People worry that "It's too late" to save our planet. We need to strike the right tone with where our people are.

A forced tone of hope, for example, can leave people feeling worse. If we say, "We can win!" and never speak to people's fear that we may not win, we can leave them in worse shape.

The Pacific Climate Warriors have been an inspiration to me on this point. Many of them live on islands that are threatened to go under as the sea levels rise. They have created a phrase: "We are not drowning, we are fighting." It's a tone of defiance — one that isn't accepting being seen as victims.

Rather than defaulting to a tone because it's what you see others do, get in touch with your people and their feelings. Let the tone reflect what's inside your people.

ADAPT TACTICS TO EXTERNAL EVENTS

Seeing how flexible we can be about tone helps us see that we can adapt tactics to fit our needs. The same tactic can be applied a lot of different ways.

When we understand that, it gives us a lot of flexibility — even if we're a tiny, local group.

I grew up in a small town. I used to believe that the big strategy decisions came from far away. It seemed like the big, urban cities or faraway networks decided what we should be doing (big global days of action or mass mobilisations).

But when we learn to *adapt* tactics, we can be more flexible. We can match the needs of the local campaigns with what's happening at the national or global levels.

For example, I'm part of a local climate justice organisation, Earth Quaker Action Team. There was a national pledge to try to stop the Keystone XL pipeline — a massive pipeline in the US that would transport up to 700,000 barrels of oil a day!

The pledge was a smart idea: Get people to commit to doing civil disobedience *before* the plans for the pipeline got approved. National organisers were encouraging people to sign up and mobilising for a big sit-in in Washington, DC.

Our local group wanted to support the efforts. We didn't want to be left out of an important, exciting national campaign. Plus, we were colleagues and friends with people leading the amazing campaign to stop the Keystone XL.

But... we also didn't want to pause our own local campaign. We were really busy stopping a local bank from investing in mountain-top-removal coal mining. We had recently made some progress on our target. And our campaign had just grown a bunch of new members. We wanted to keep the energy going.

What to do? We needed a way to marry our local action with the national action. And we found it by turning to the Act-Recruit-Train cycle.

We needed to "Train" the new people we had just recruited. So we connected the national campaign's ask (the pledge to do civil disobedience) to a training for people in our campaign.

We had people publicly sign the pledge, then did a practice civil disobedience action targeting the local office of the Keystone XL target (the US State Department). We swept their offices (to try to clean out the corruption) until police escorted us out of the building. We coupled the action with a long debrief to teach people about the theory of nonviolence and why we were a nonviolent direct action campaign.

It was a win/win.

The national groups got more signatures, more attention, and more people who were skilled in direct action. And our local campaign got a boost from new people who joined just because we were doing something on Keystone and used this moment to build new skills for our newer group members.

There are rarely perfect matches where everything goes smoothly. And sometimes it's okay to make the decision to *not* be part of every national action *or* to drop some actions in your local activities. Those may be the right choices, too![20]

In Occupy, local groups experimented with changing the location. When Occupy launched in the US, some cities like Mineapolis and Atlanta launched variations. They would occupy homes where the big banks were foreclosing people. The tactic became a practical way to help people keep their homes.

The concept here is important: Make actions yours. Fit them with your local needs and situation.

This is especially important as local climate disasters strike and we need to adapt.

Learning this skill helps us organise more successful actions. And that presents its own challenges.

PLAN TWO ACTIONS AHEAD

After a successful action, the most common question I get is: "So what's the next action?"

As an organiser, I hate not having an answer to this. It's a wasted opportunity when we have to reply: "We'll let you know. Look out on Facebook."

How much better to have this answer: "Save next Friday for another action!" (or, at least, "Come to our meeting next week to help us figure it out").

Because of this, I recommend that groups try to plan *two* actions ahead of time. That way, when the first happens, the second is already planned.

The power of tactics as part of a strategy really comes into focus when we string them together. Each tactic can build on the other to increase its power.

Actions that are announced far enough ahead of time also give time for our opponents to worry, too. Organiser Saul Alinsky used to say: "The threat is usually more terrifying than the thing itself."

Here's an example of how these work together.

Years ago, I worked on an unusually planned campaign. This campaign shows the elements we've been talking about — spectrum of allies, recruiting outside your circle, the upside-down triangle. This plan was adapted by several generations of organisers, including Canadian nonviolent strategist Philippe Duhamel. It's been taken and adapted by other campaigns (maybe yours will use it!).

We had two giant unwanted casinos proposed for our city. The community was locked out at every step. No public input. No engagement. We were expected to roll over and give up.

We wanted more than a rally. We wanted a way to embed our movement's values in our action.

We decided on our target: the politicians who had approved casinos. And we looked at the pillars of support. The casinos had basically everyone in their corner: city officials, state officials, media, judges, academics… just about everyone with any power. It seemed hopeless. And it was all happening so fast we didn't have time to process the information. (Sound familiar?)

So we set up a dilemma. We gave a one-month notice that we wanted the release of all the documents that had been kept secret. These documents included site plans, social impact studies, environmental plans, architectural renderings, and economic studies. "We are asking for all these documents to be made public by December 1 at high noon," we announced. "If they are not, then we will be forced to get them ourselves, going to the Gaming Control Board headquarters and performing a citizens' document search to liberate them."

We created a timeline of actions. And because we were standing for transparency, we made it public for everyone to see. Here's a quick review of how our actions went down:

October 30 • Trick or Treat: Deliver Ultimatum

We brought Halloween treats and magnifying glasses to the mayor and City Council. Oh — and we used the mayor's fax machine (it's ours, after all!) to fax our demand to the Governor that all documents be made public by December 1 or we would be forced to search for them ourselves.

A few press outlets covered us. Only five or six people joined this action (and, to be fair, two of them were my roommates).

November 13 • Gaming Board "Public" Hearings

We tried to avoid responding to the opposition's timeline too much. Sticking to our timeline made us stronger. But they were holding a big hearing, and we figured people would attend. So we planned an action. We jumped out with magnifying glasses and playfully tried to search all the casino executives and lawyers going into the meeting ("Do you have the documents?" we asked, with our magnifying glasses aloft).

Press started to ask us serious questions. And a few allies started to listen when we asked them for their support. Two other people agreed to do the document search with us.

November 20 • Delivery of Petitions and Washing Windows for Transparency
We went to the Gaming Control Board offices… to wash their windows. You know — to help them become more transparent. (We delivered petitions, too.)

This was a lot of fun — and around this time, people started to get excited about what we were doing. Our tone was light and playful. And our actions were getting good press coverage. We used the press as a way to pressure our target (we urged reporters to ask them tough questions). And we kept knocking on neighbours' doors to join us. Most had now heard about us and, if they were not supportive, were curious.

November 23 • Thanksgiving to Whistleblowers of the World
We wrote letters of support, encouraging people inside the Gaming Control Board to become whistleblowers. We gave them brown envelopes to send back to us with the documents.

Honestly, we barely pulled this off. The timeline was too quick (just three days after the other action? I would never do it so fast again!). But at least we followed through on our commitment.

December 1 • End of Ultimatum
We had stated publicly that if the documents were not made public, then we would be forced to announce our intention to search for them ourselves.

But note that on this day, we didn't *do* the action. We just had a press conference. We were using time to our advantage — making our opponents more nervous ("What comes next?"). And the time helped our reluctant allies. This was the first day any politicians started to endorse our campaign.

December 10 • Training in Nonviolent Document Search
Training is so important! We learn things — and the training was a chance to recruit more people. Three new people signed up to do the action after seeing the training!

December 11 • Nonviolent Document Search
Our action was our message. We attempted to go up to their offices and liberate the documents.

The dilemma placed our opposition in a double-bind. If the Gaming Control Board kept the documents secret, they confirmed public suspicions that they were hiding something nefarious. If they released the documents, we achieved a win for transparency. Heads we win, tails you lose.

And what happened?

The Gaming Control Board did not want to give us the documents. They called the police, who arrested fourteen of us (we were charged with minor rule breaking).

But in the following days, people came out in support of us. More elected officials. More union members. Environmentalists began to see the damage these casinos would cause. And timid politicians, like weather vanes, pointed our way.

The campaign for transparency came to a close when the Gaming Control Board released almost every document we asked for.[21]

But campaigns don't end there. Campaigns create new campaigns — and it was a multi-year struggle for us to win, just like it will be for us on climate change.

And in the campaign, you can see how these pieces come together: setting a tone (ours was playful), adapting tactics to external dates (integrating the hearing with our schedule), and planning tactics ahead of time (if we hadn't, I'm sure we would not have been able to keep going).

One more theory about tactics will help as we find the right tactics for us.

DILEMMA DEMONSTRATIONS

You have probably seen groups block roads or do sit-ins at politicians' offices. Sometimes they work, and sometimes they don't — that's true for any tactic.

But one thing that often is likely to turn off our spectrum of allies is when we *get in their way but don't seem to have a legitimate reason why*. We know that our cause is right — but it matters to our campaign how our potential allies see our tactics.

I often think of a time I watched fellow protestors blocking traffic when the Republican Party was visiting my hometown. The protestors wanted to create a disruption. But the people being disrupted were fellow Philadelphians. One shouted from her window the sentiment of many people in my city, "I hate the Republicans, too — but I need to go pick up my kids."

The tactic didn't have its intended effect.

We can't eliminate this possibility. But we can reduce it.

Perhaps one of the core lessons to learn for movements wishing to engage in confrontation is how to create *dilemma demonstrations*.

Dilemma demonstrations are actions that force the target to either let you do what you want, or to be shown as unreasonable as they stop you from doing it.

Dilemma demonstrations provide an advantage either way the opponent responds. The Civil Rights sit-in activists go into a luncheonette and demand a cup of coffee. If they get the cup of coffee, great — another discriminatory practice falls! If they get arrested or beaten up instead, the activists still gain an advantage. The violence that underlies racism is exposed, and the movement grows.

The secret in designing a dilemma is that the campaigners need to create an advantage for themselves no matter what happens. It wouldn't work if the demonstrators couldn't create an advantage either way — if the sit-in organisers, for example, regarded getting the coffee (or being beaten and jailed) as a defeat.

In the transparency campaign against the casinos, the document search action was *doing* the thing we wanted done.

This is at the heart of most powerful direct actions.

These are vastly different from tactics like rallies, marches, or vigils, which are symbolic in nature. And they're different from other direct actions like a generic blockade, which impedes motorists but whose goal isn't made clear by the action. Dilemma demonstrations take a piece of our vision and implement it.

That gives them *action logic*. Action logic is the degree to which the outsider can understand the meaning of the action because its message is embedded in the action itself, not in a sign.

Dilemma demonstrations have been used to great effect:

♦   Faced with a giant pipeline being built through their territories, Standing Rock Sioux elder LaDonna Brave Bull Allard established a camp. The camp was a physical barrier blocking the pipeline, but it was more than that. It was a camp for cultural preservation and spiritual resistance. The camp became an international symbol, even as the actual camp was also a physical bulwark against the pipeline.

- Dilemma demonstrations have been done again in the same campaign against the Keystone XL pipeline. Indigenous communities, landowners, farmers, along with supporting organizations, launched Solar XL. This time they are putting up active solar panels ("a wave of renewable energy resistance") directly in the route of the proposed pipeline. In each case, the opponents have a dilemma: wipe out a camp or solar panels — or let them block the pipeline?

- Gandhi was a tactical genius and created a brilliant dilemma demonstration. The British occupation of India oppressed his people in many ways. He wanted to find an action that could be replicated in other places, would be meaningful, and would challenge British power. He knew salt was something everyone needed to live. And the British made a lot of money because they were the only ones allowed to sell salt. So he began a whole campaign of people making their own salt. If they had been allowed to make salt, they would have been delighted. But the British empire chose repression — and that shredded the idea that the British had a right to rule India and hastened their departure.

- Neo-Nazis regularly marched in a small town in Germany. The population was not happy about it. But counter-protesting them never amounted to much. So activist group Recht gegen Rechts (Right against Right) came up with a different strategy — an "involuntary walkathon." For each meter the Neo-Nazis marched, money was donated to an organisation that specialised in helping former Neo-Nazis get away from that movement. The dilemma was clear: If they chose to march, it created funds. But if they chose not to march, well, that's what the town wanted all along[22].

- A neighbourhood in my city of Philadelphia didn't have trash or recycling picked up. They organised a neighbourhood trash pick-up and sent a bill for the services they provided. When it wasn't paid, they dumped next week's trash in front of City Hall. The city found money to do trash collection the next week!

◆ The Pacific Climate Warriors found a dilemma demonstration by reaching back to their old traditions to save their islands. With support from elders, they built hand-carved traditional canoes. Warriors from 12 different nations took those canoes to Newcastle, Australia. That's one of the largest coal ports in the world. For a day, the warriors took the canoes and blockaded the coal port — confronting gigantic coal ships that pass through the channel. Their action was their message: the future is rooted in our past traditions, not more coal.

When we manage to find dilemma demonstrations, we strengthen our campaigns. These actions are impossible for our opposition to ignore — and force them to make a difficult choice (repress us, or allow the movement to make a concrete achievement).

NEXT STEPS

Get tools for creative tactics in your group, like "Action Accordion" and "How to create a campaign plan: the paper plate challenge" — and find handouts on creating powerful actions with strong action logic at trainings.350.org.

Learn more about these concepts in the online skill-up course "Advanced Campaigning" at trainings.350.org/online-skillups

Chapter 5: Closing

MANY OF US ARE ALREADY experiencing the effects of the climate crisis. Outside my window, I can see how a rising sea is impacting my river's tides. Our uncommonly warm season disturbed bird migratory patterns. Heat waves are rising and threatening the health of the elderly where I live.

These are disturbing facts, because worse is coming. Even if we somehow managed to win quickly, the impacts of what we have already done to the Earth are far-reaching.

Because of that, I come back to what I think are the building blocks of movements: *Relationships*. Relationships with each other. With ourselves. With our movement elders and familial spirits of those before us. With our fellow plant and animal life. With our Mother Earth.

Movements are at their best when they are growing love. They are an *act* of collective hope in the face of long odds.

In our groups and campaigns, we build relationships. These webs and fabrics of communities are how we will see this crisis through. They will be networks to adjust, transition, and hold onto resistance, even as individuals may shift in and out of roles. Our tenderness and care for each other during each step binds us closer.

To do that, we have to remain loving inside ourselves. It's important that we set healthy boundaries for our spirit so the fast pace, urgency, and demands of life do not overwhelm us. Like skin is a boundary between us and the rest of the world, we need boundaries — with news, with our social media sources. That means taking breaks from social media. And being conscious of what we do after listening to news so it's not bombarding us all times of the day.

Boundaries are good. And we need openness — to keep opening ourselves up to those we know who are being impacted by the climate crisis. Our hearts must remain open — and extend that love to all who are suffering. That includes seeking out stories of how others have resisted injustice. Studying oppression does not make us stronger; it's studying *resistance* that teaches us the skills we need.[23]

In studying resistance, we learn about how people have found *balance* to do this. There was a range of how the Mongolian students acted. Some denied their parents' request to stop and just focus on school work. They decided the moment was too important. Others went in waves — supporting big pushes and then pulling back to stay on top of school work. And each searched out the rhythm that was right for them and their situation. Movements need so many roles — there are so many ways to participate.

These and other things protect our spirits for the long haul. The urgency of now means we must ground deeply. We should keep sharing what we are learning with others — so that we can support each other to find our ways through.

It's when we are grounded that we step most strongly into building campaigns that speak to soul and love and spirit. We move the rock of activated social values and the spectrum of allies when we come from our hearts. We find those creative tactics not when we're buried in our minds, but when we're brimming with creativity.

Therefore, you matter in the course of this. So please go and use this book. Go help our climate get better. Join all of us trying to stop the tide of this impending climate crisis. And keep loving deeply, widely and bravely.

Notes

Find additional resources, tools, and materials at: trainings.350.org.

---

[1] Peter Ackerman and Jack DuVall, *A Force More Powerful: A Century of Nonviolent Conflict* (New York: St. Martin's Press, 2000)

[2] Get the upside-down triangle (and more strategy tools) at Trainings.350.org.

[3] Srdja Popovic et al., *Nonviolent Struggle: 50 Crucial Points* (Belgrade, Serbia: CANVAS, 2006), www.usip.org/sites/default/files/nonviolent_eng.pdf.

[4] For more facts on climate change, watch "Do the Math" at math.350.org or take the online courses on Climate Science at Trainings.350.org/online-skillups.

[5] Learn more about this campaign in an interactive online course — Introduction to Campaigning 101 — at Trainings.350.org/online-skillups.

[6] "The June 16 Soweto Youth Uprising," *South African History Online,* May 21, 2013, https://www.sahistory.org.za/topic/june-16-soweto-youth-uprising.

[7] Get the spectrum of allies (and more strategy tools) at Trainings.350.org.

[8] Learn more about this Brazilian fracking campaign in an online course — Introduction to Campaigning 101 — at Trainings.350.org/online-skillups.

[9] For a very worthwhile long book, read Taylor Branch's *Parting the Waters: America in the King Years* (New York, New York: Simon and Schuster, 1988).

[10] More on Act-Recruit-Train model: gofossilfree.org/usa/divestment-guide-train/.

[11] This story is in the handout "Increase Your Volunteers' Involvement: Using the Ladder of Engagement" at Trainings.350.org.

[12] Get the ladder of engagement (and more organising tools) at Trainings.350.org.

[13] Collected movement lessons: Marcel Taminto, et al, *Beautiful Rising: Creative Resistance from the Global South* (New York & London. OR Books, 2017).

[14] Learn more about Otpor's movement-building in *Bringing Down a Dictator,* directed by Steve York (Washington, DC: A Force More Powerful Films, 2001), DVD.

[15] These stories come from 350's case studies they call Organising Story-telling Labs. "How to Recruit More People" at trainings.350.org/labs.

[16] "Making Escalated Actions Bold and Safe Despite Repression" at: trainings.350.org/labs (see above).

[17] "How to Influence a Political 'Frenemy'," at: trainings.350.org/labs (see above).

[18] "How to win by thinking like your opponent" at: trainings.350.org/labs (see above).

[19] "How France fought to keep it in the ground" at trainings.350.org/labs (see above).

[20] Learn Earth Quaker Action Team's campaign strategy in George Lakey, *How We Win: A Guide to Nonviolent Direct Action Campaigning* (Melville House Books, 2018) or read their website: www.eqat.org.

[21] Read more about this campaign in a thrilling page-turner: Daniel Hunter, *Strategy & Soul* (Philadelphia: Hyrax Books, 2013) www.strategyandsoul.org.

[22] This and other cool tactics are described in Actipedia, actipedia.org/project/german-town-tricks-neo-nazis-marching-against-themselves.

[23] Find strategies for grounding in the midst of crises: www.findingsteadyground.com.

About the Contributors

Daniel Hunter is Associate Director of Global Trainings with 350.org. He has spent his life supporting grassroots activists all over the globe to express their full hearts in action.

He wrote a fun, true-life story of how campaigning looks like in *Strategy and Soul*. He's also authored *Building a Movement to End the New Jim Crow* and is a contributor to the books *Beautiful Trouble* and *We Have Not Been Moved*.

He's launched several websites to teach people about social change, including FindingSteadyGround.com, the Global Nonviolent Database, and most recently Trainings.350.org.

J'ziah Cook (artist) is a visual artist who loves scary movies and art and hates spicy food. He also loves (and hates) his school, University of the Arts in Philadelphia.

You can see more of his artwork @virgo_artistry on Instagram. Or you can email him at jziahabundantcook@gmail.com.

Daphne Philippoussis (artist) is a visual artist who loves exploring the arts — either in music or fine arts. She loves Margaret Atwood and rain hitting her window. She will begin studying at Tyler School of Art at Temple University.

You can see more of her artwork @killedmykactus. Or you can email her at dphilippoussis@icloud.com.

Greta Thunberg (foreword) is an activist who started protesting her Swedish government's lack of sufficient action on the climate crisis. She started Skolstrejk för klimatet ("School strike for the climate"), where she walked out of school and sat outside of Parliament.

Others have followed her actions and in so doing she helped spark a global movement of hundreds of thousands of students joining her climate walkouts.